The Coloring book

of

"Princess in Moon" storybook

Design and finish your style storybook now.

Author: Floyd Franklin

Illustrator: Miao Lin

This book contains two parts and an appendix.

Part One

It is the draft of a storybook, "Princess in Moon."
You can paint the book as you like.
Or you also can follow the sketch of the draft to practice the skill of sketch of a storybook.
You also can add the color for each page. And you can buy the paperback book of "Princess in Moon" for comparing.
Maybe you will find your color style is better than we do!

Part Two

Blank page leaves for your style of design and sketch of all new drafts of this story.

Appendix

The Appendix provides the story of "Princess in Moon."
You can read the story before you start to paint.

PART ONE

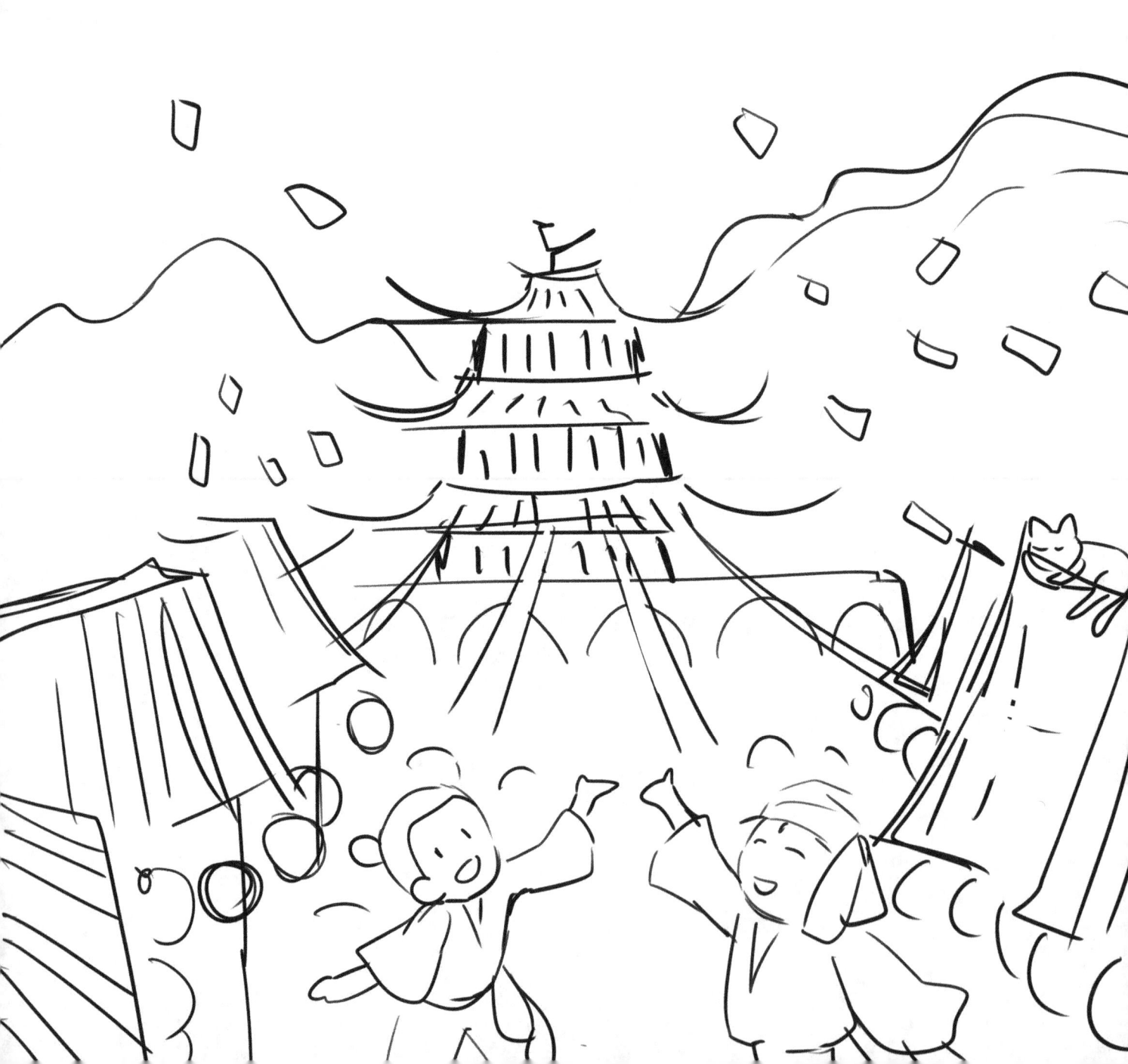

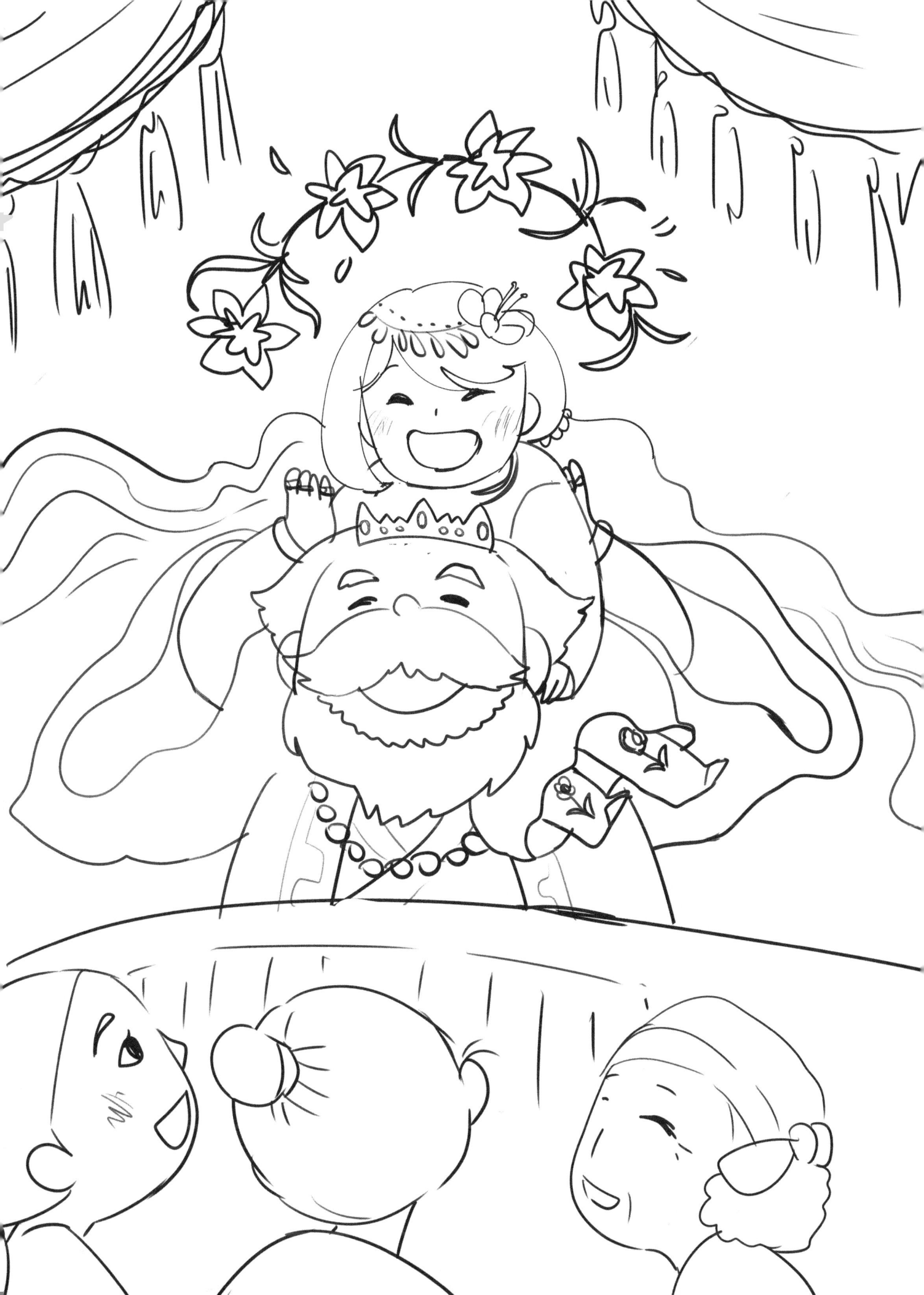

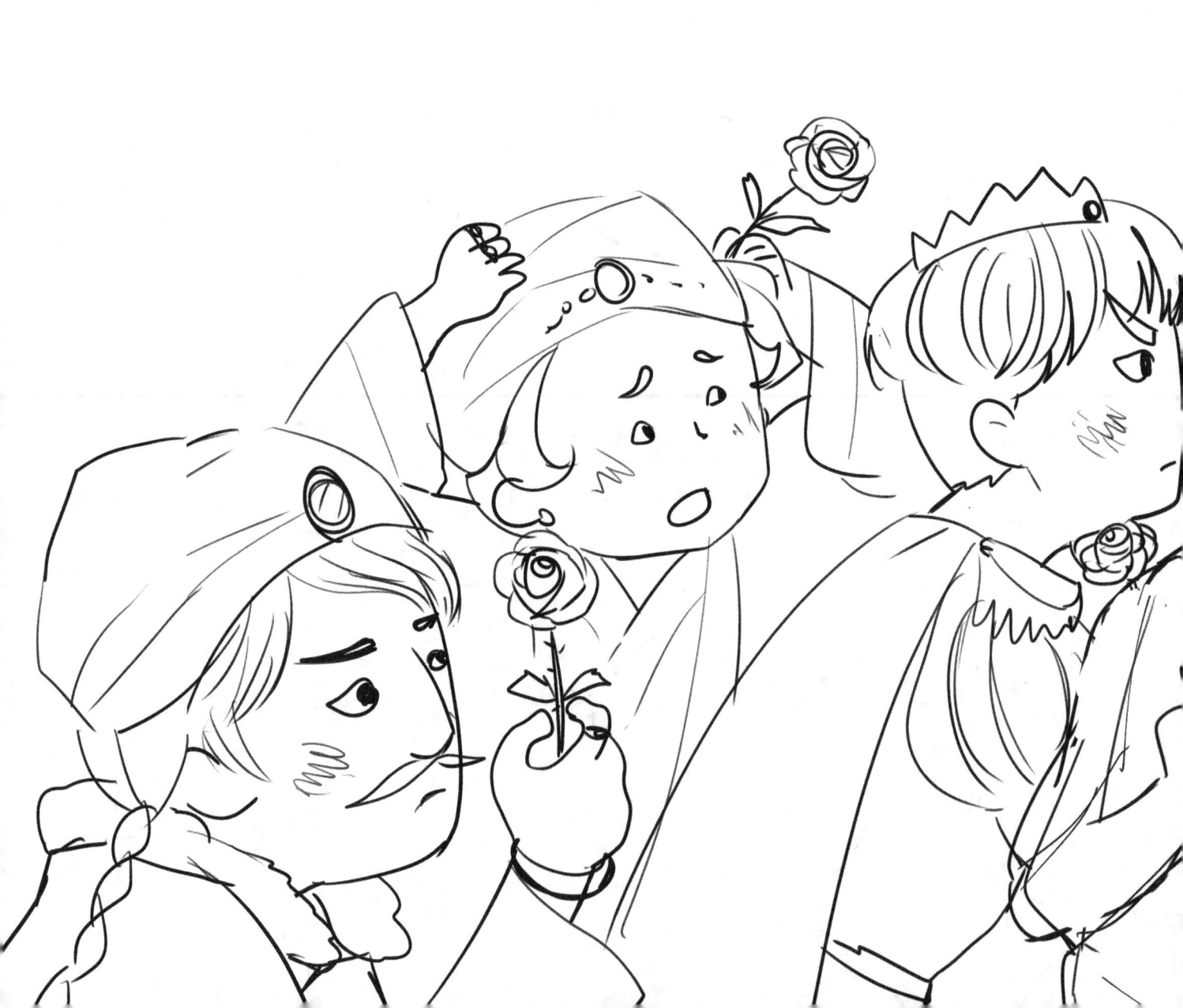

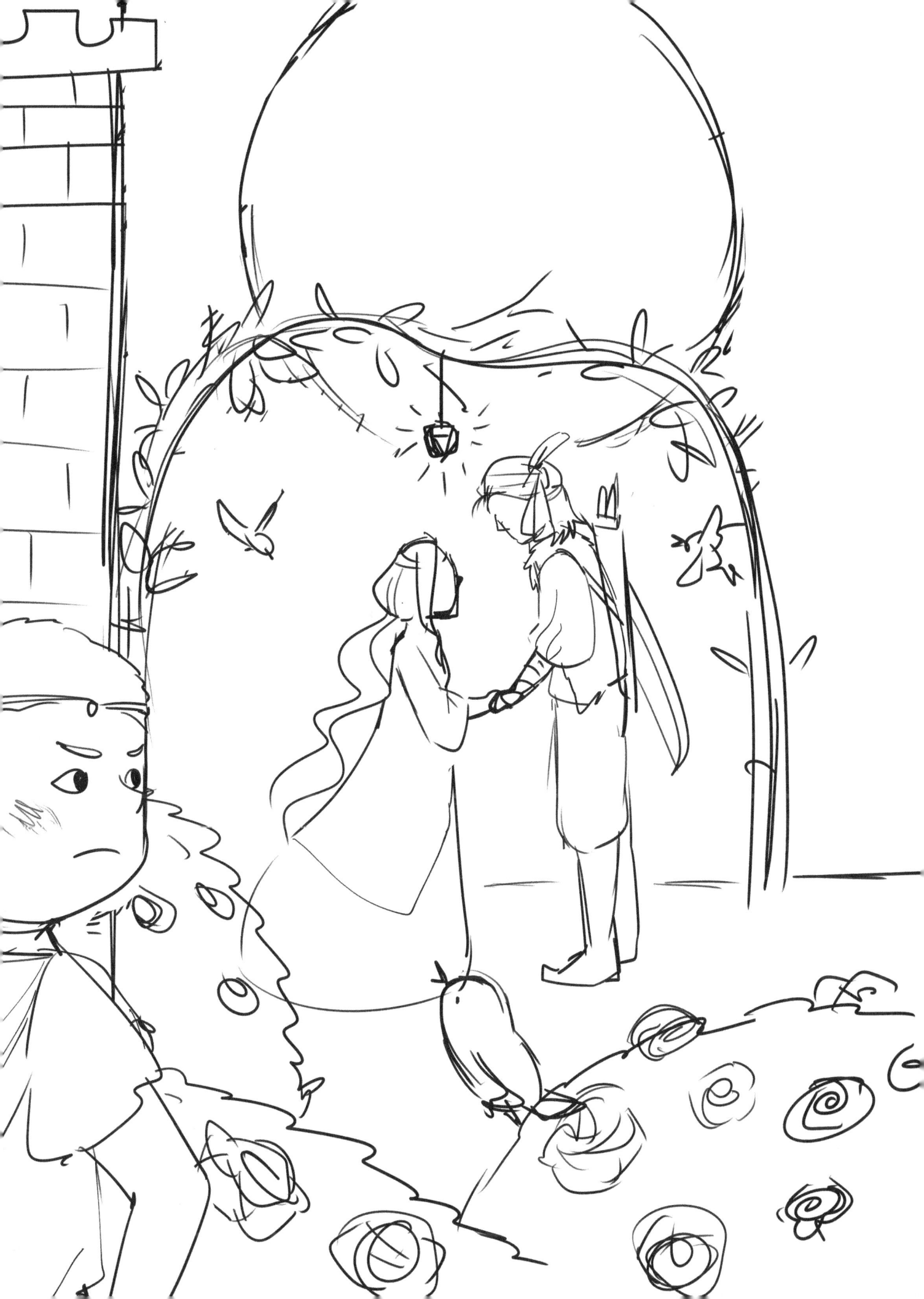

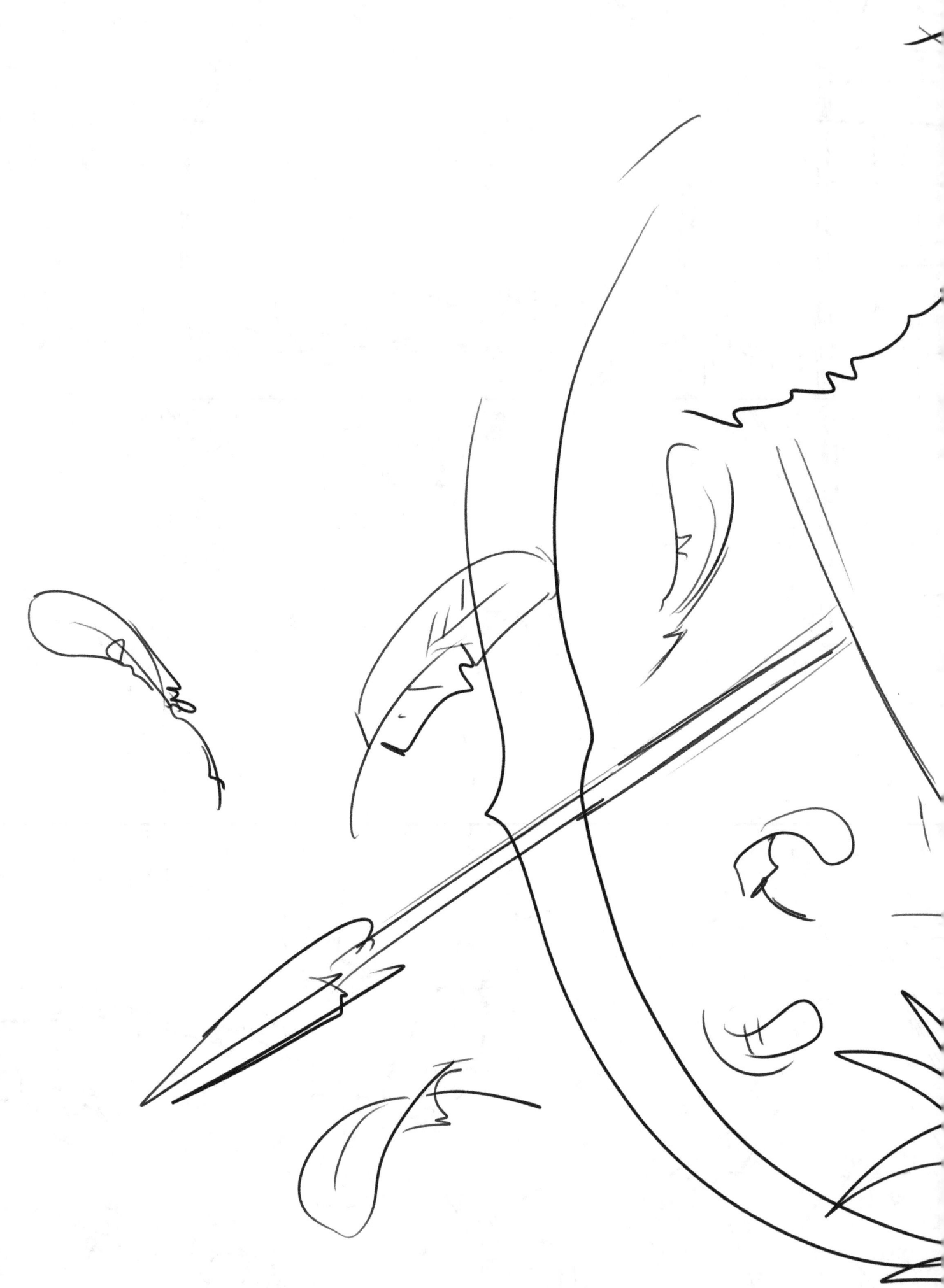

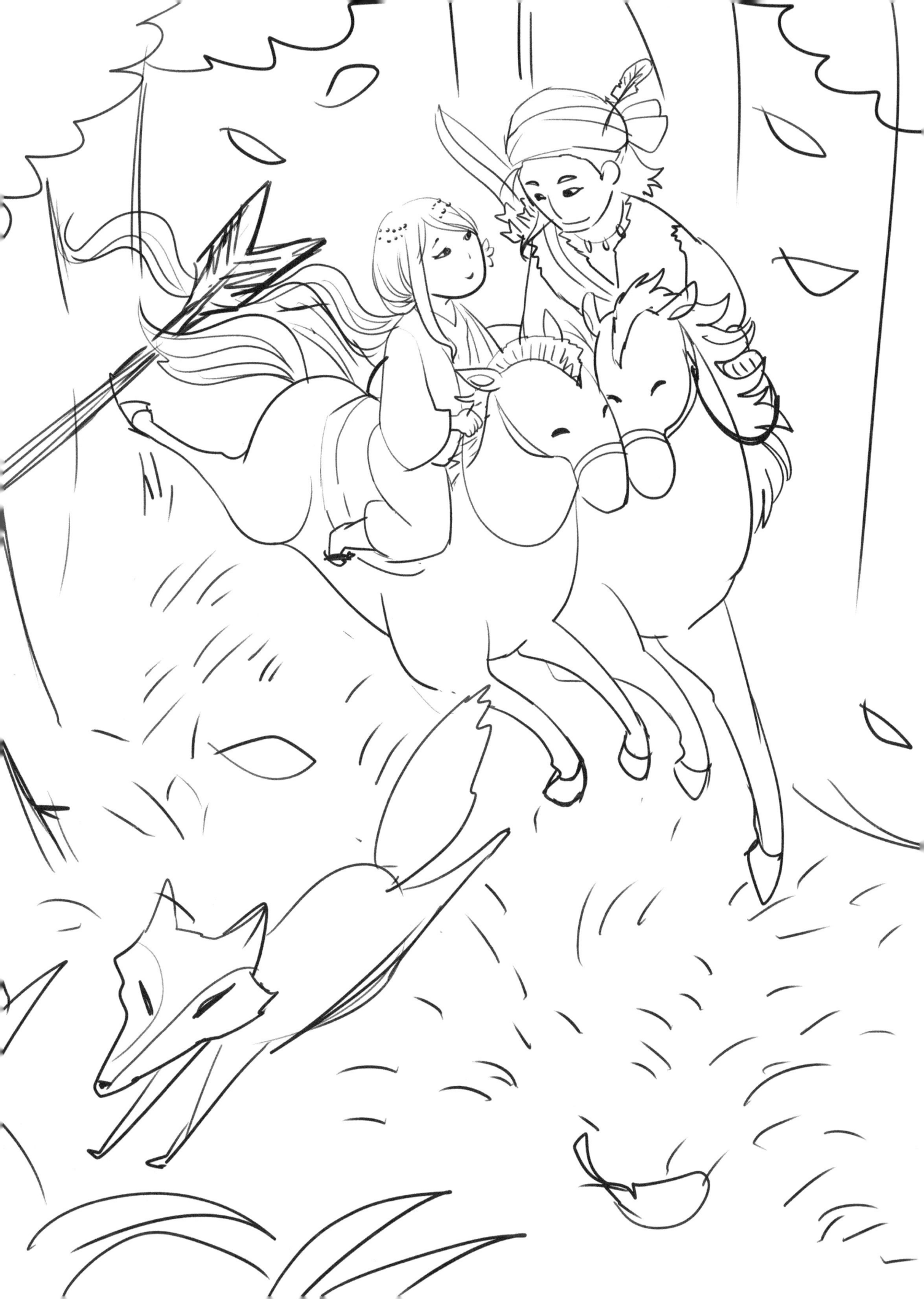

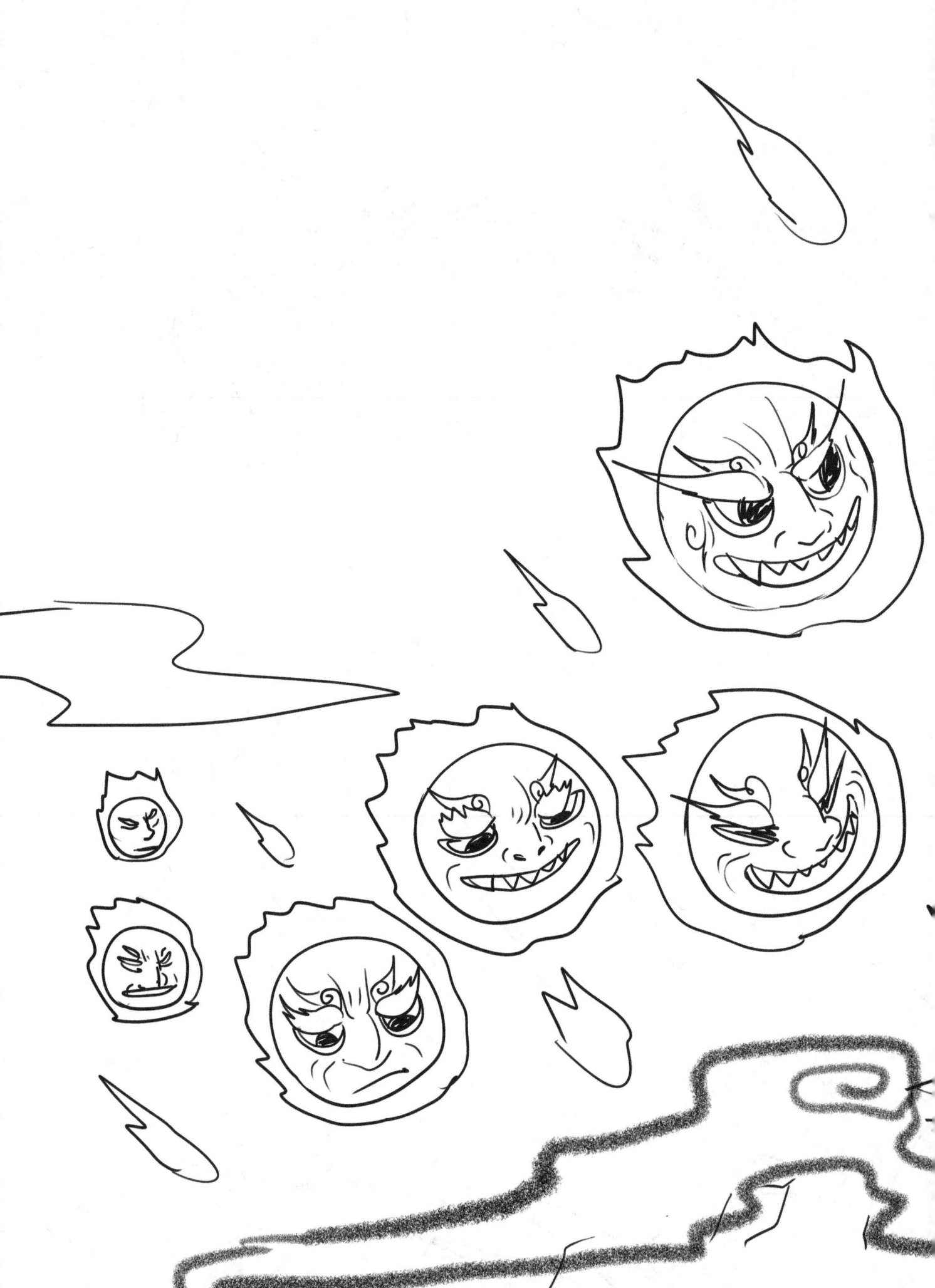

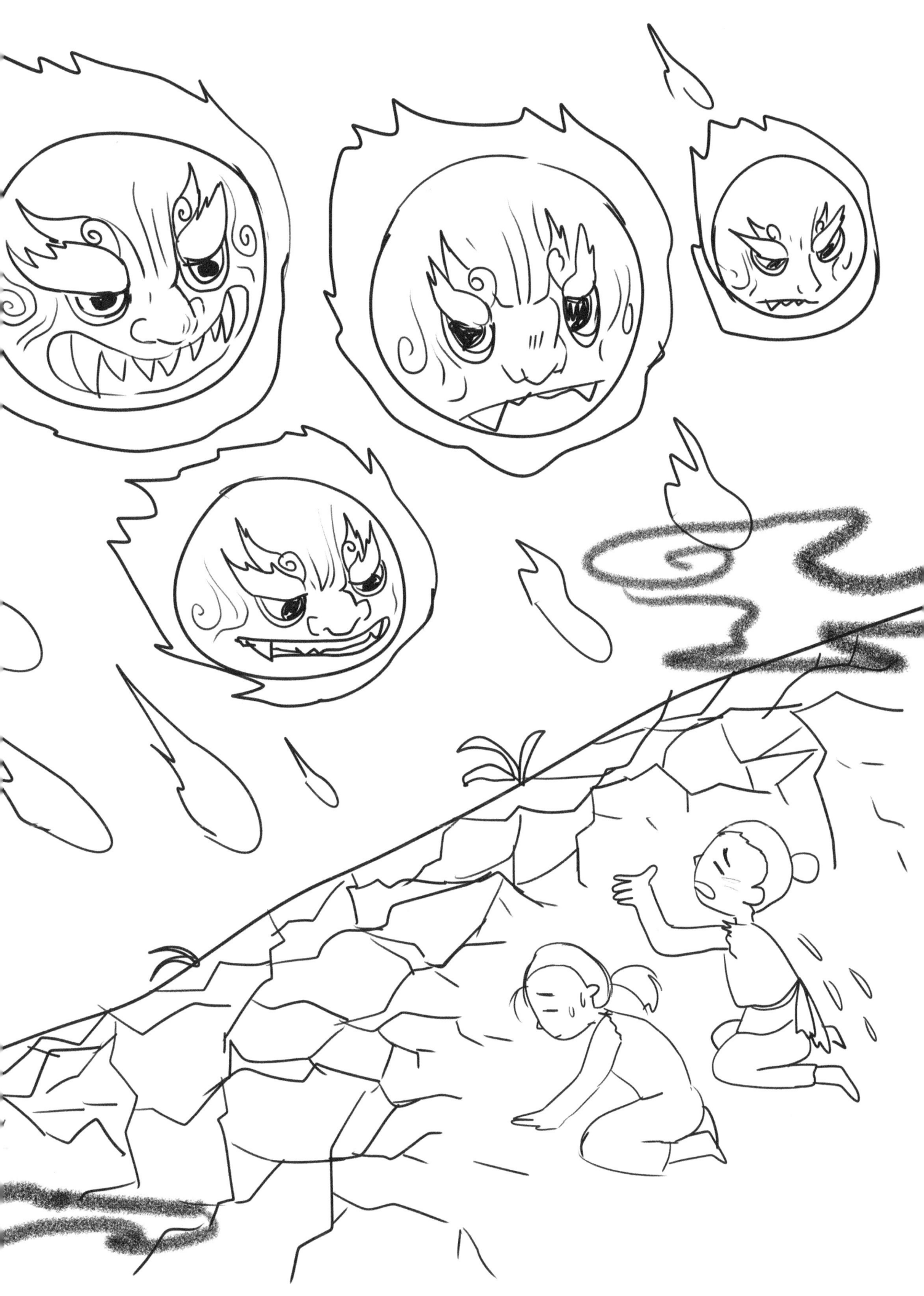

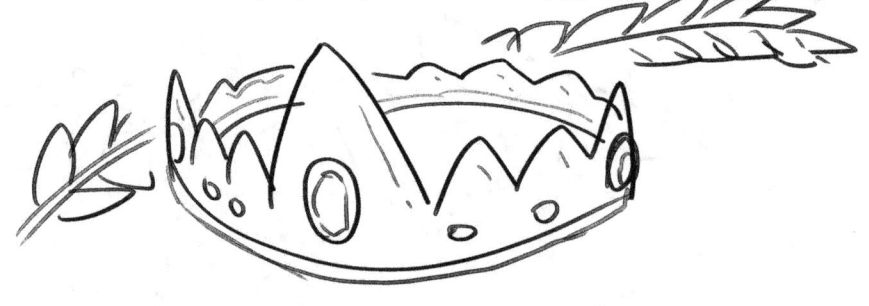

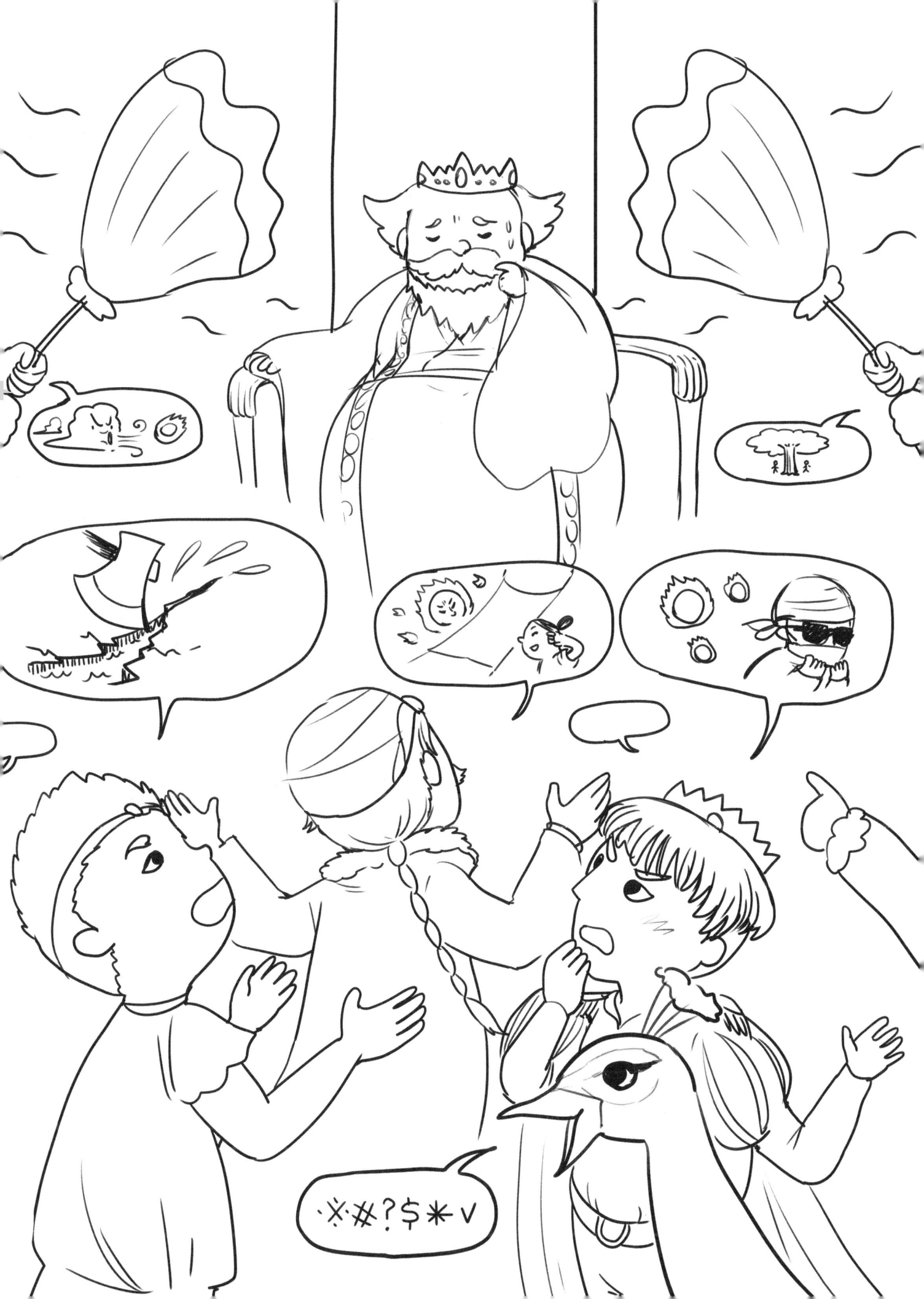

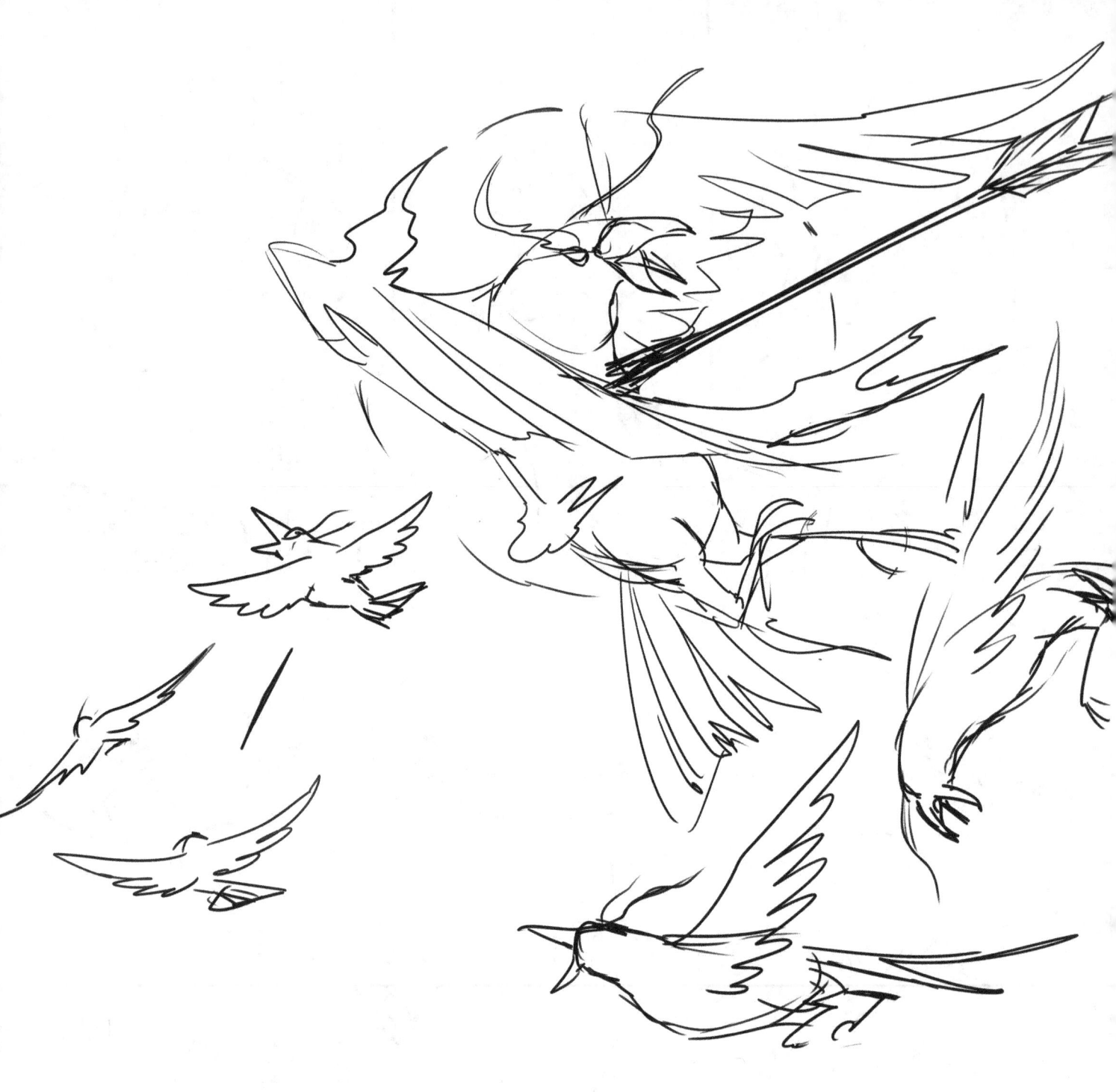

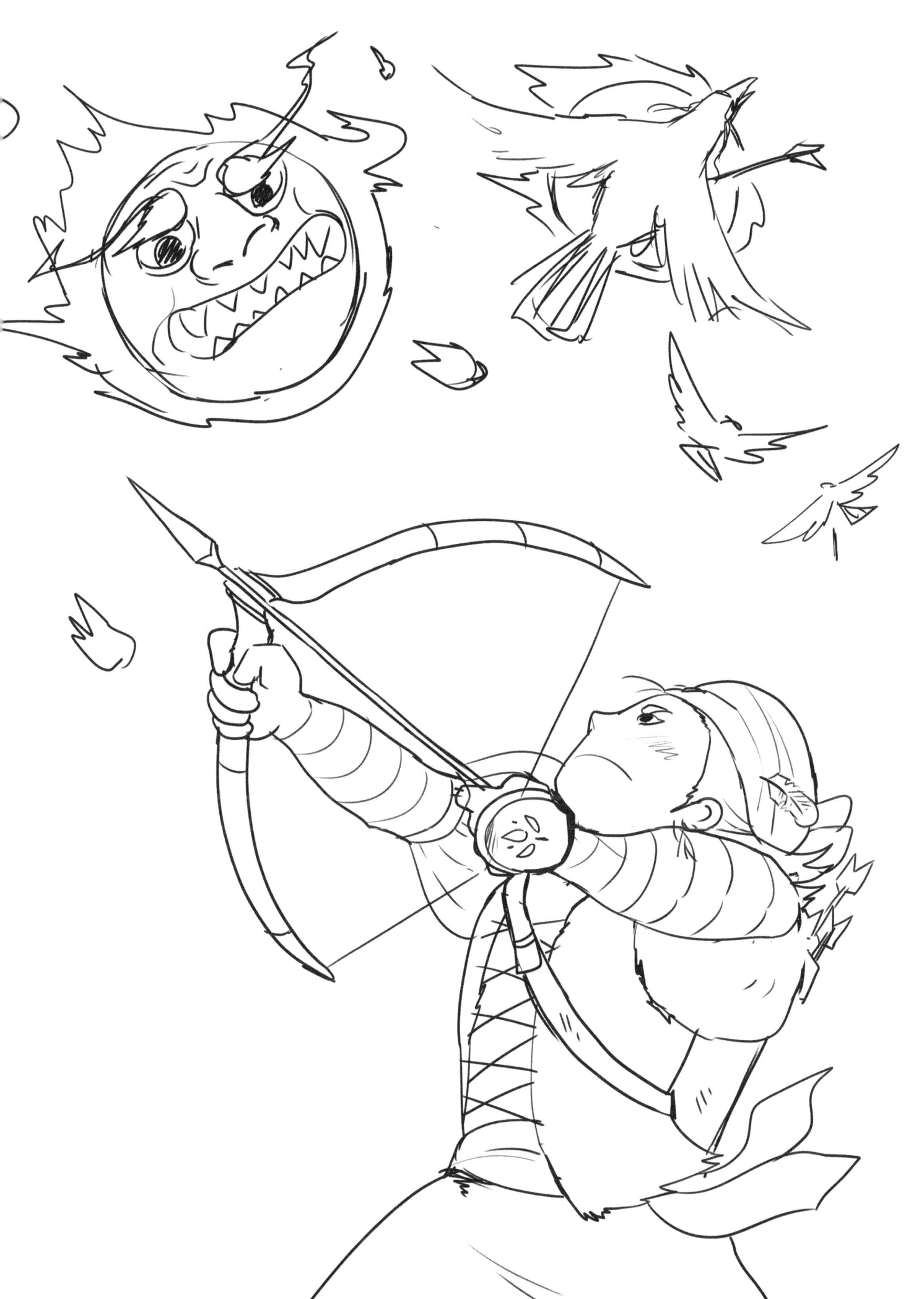

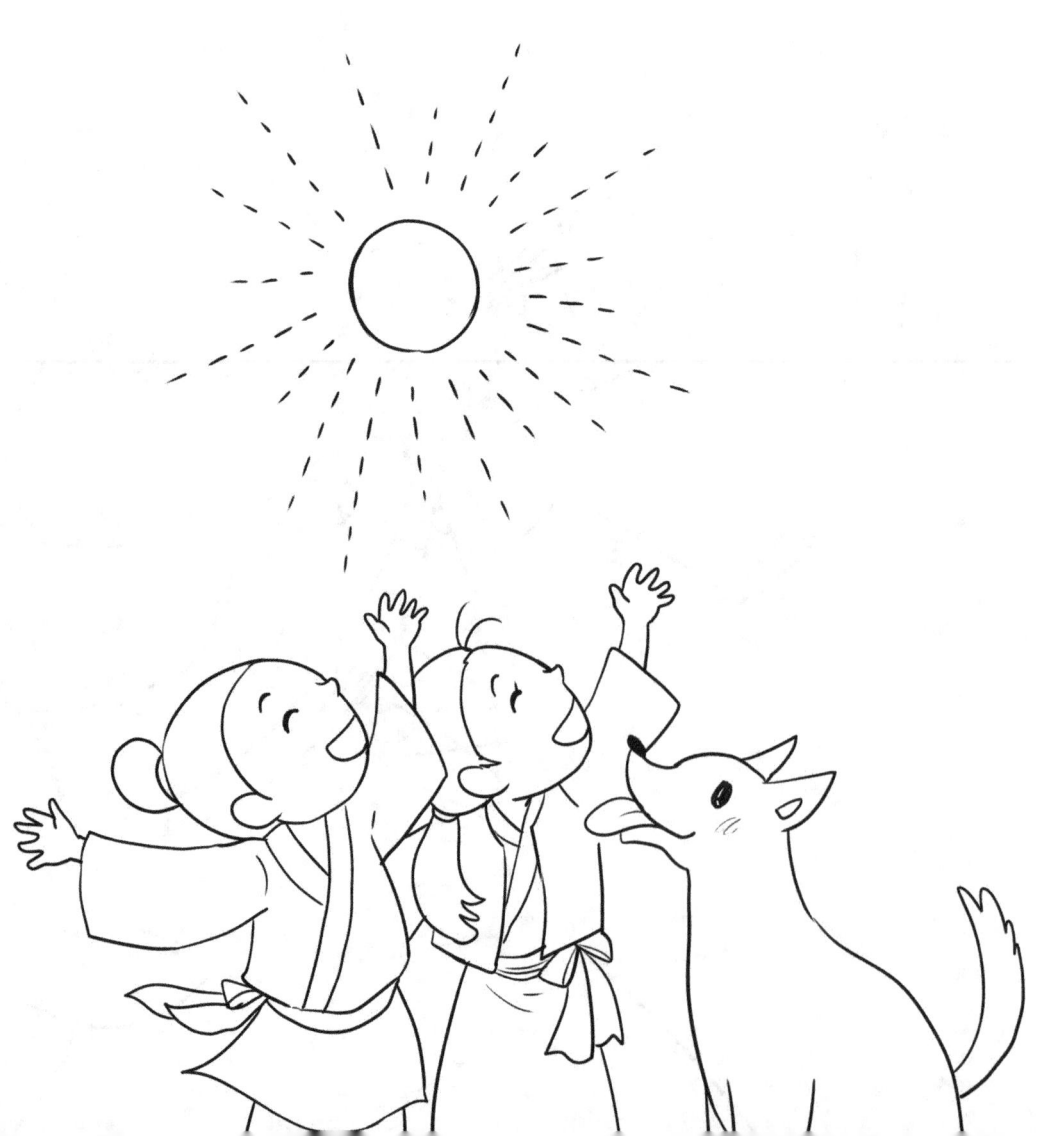

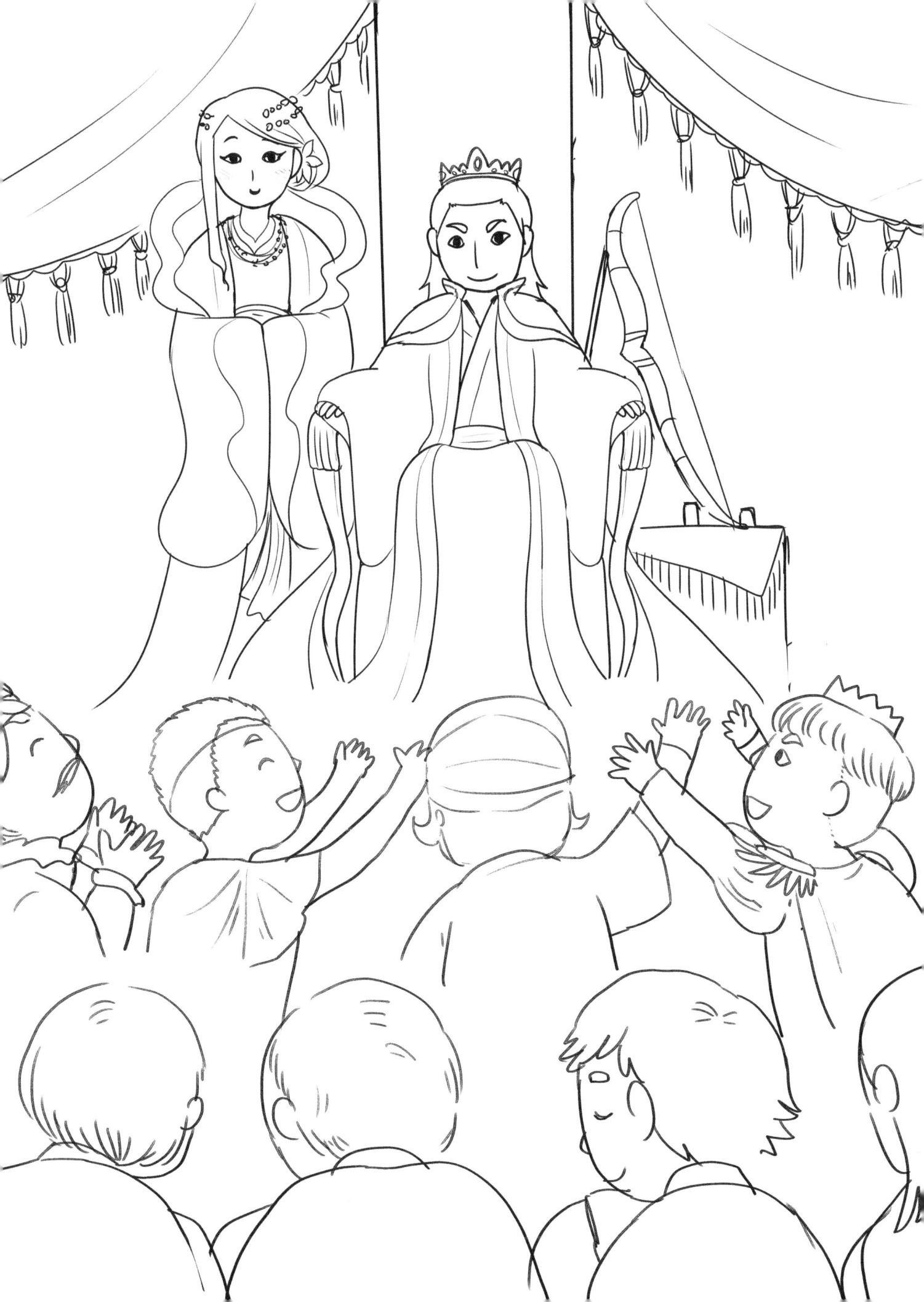

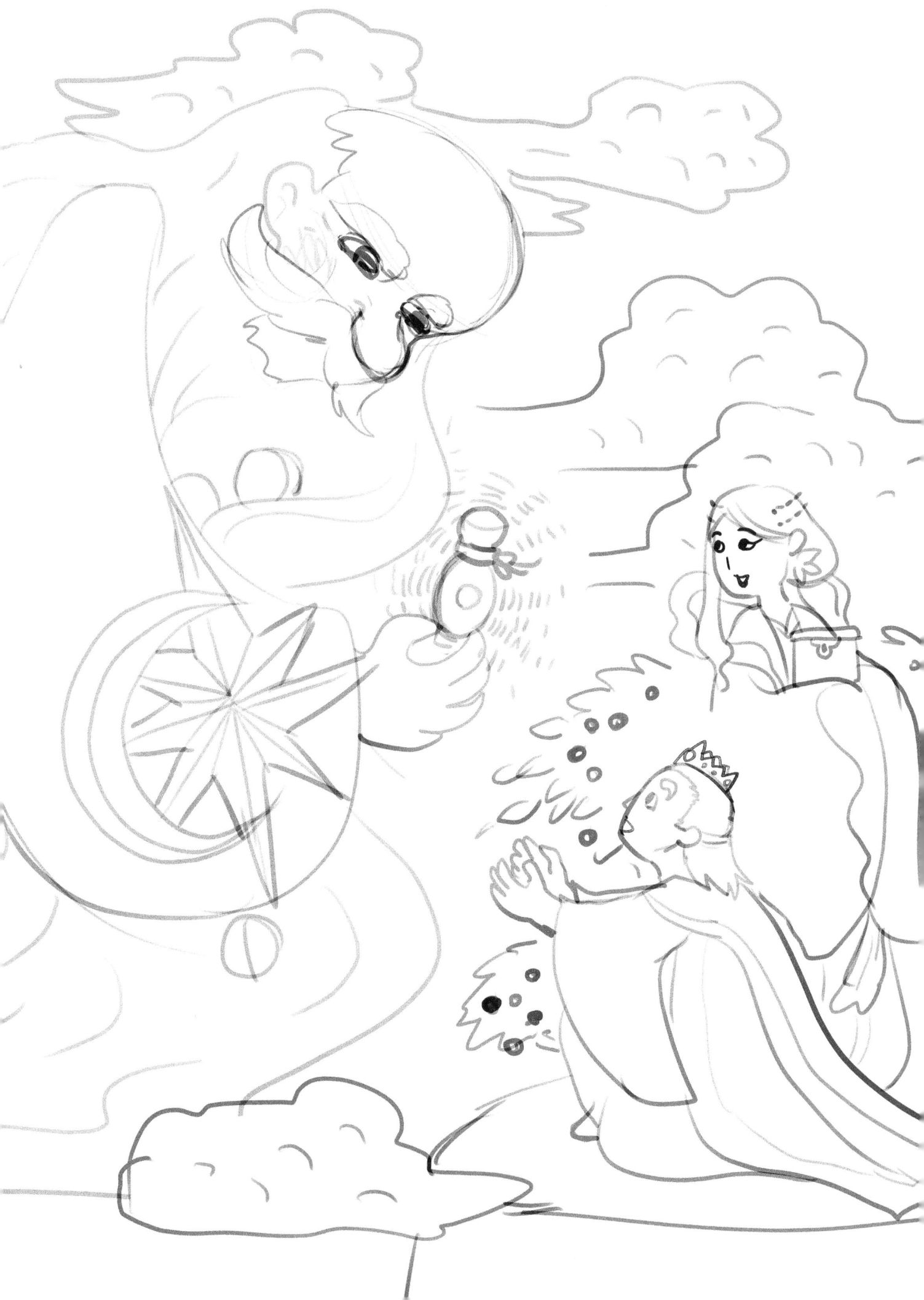

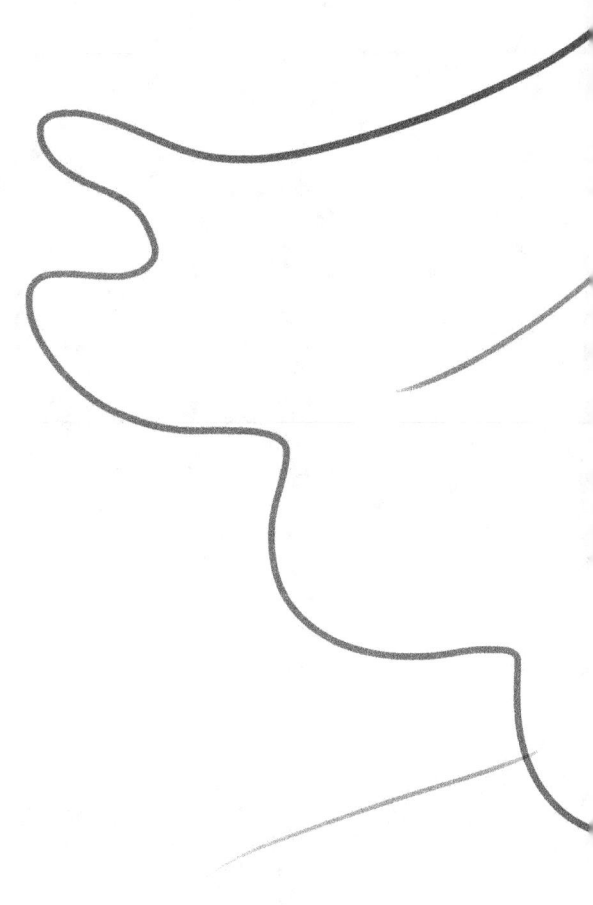

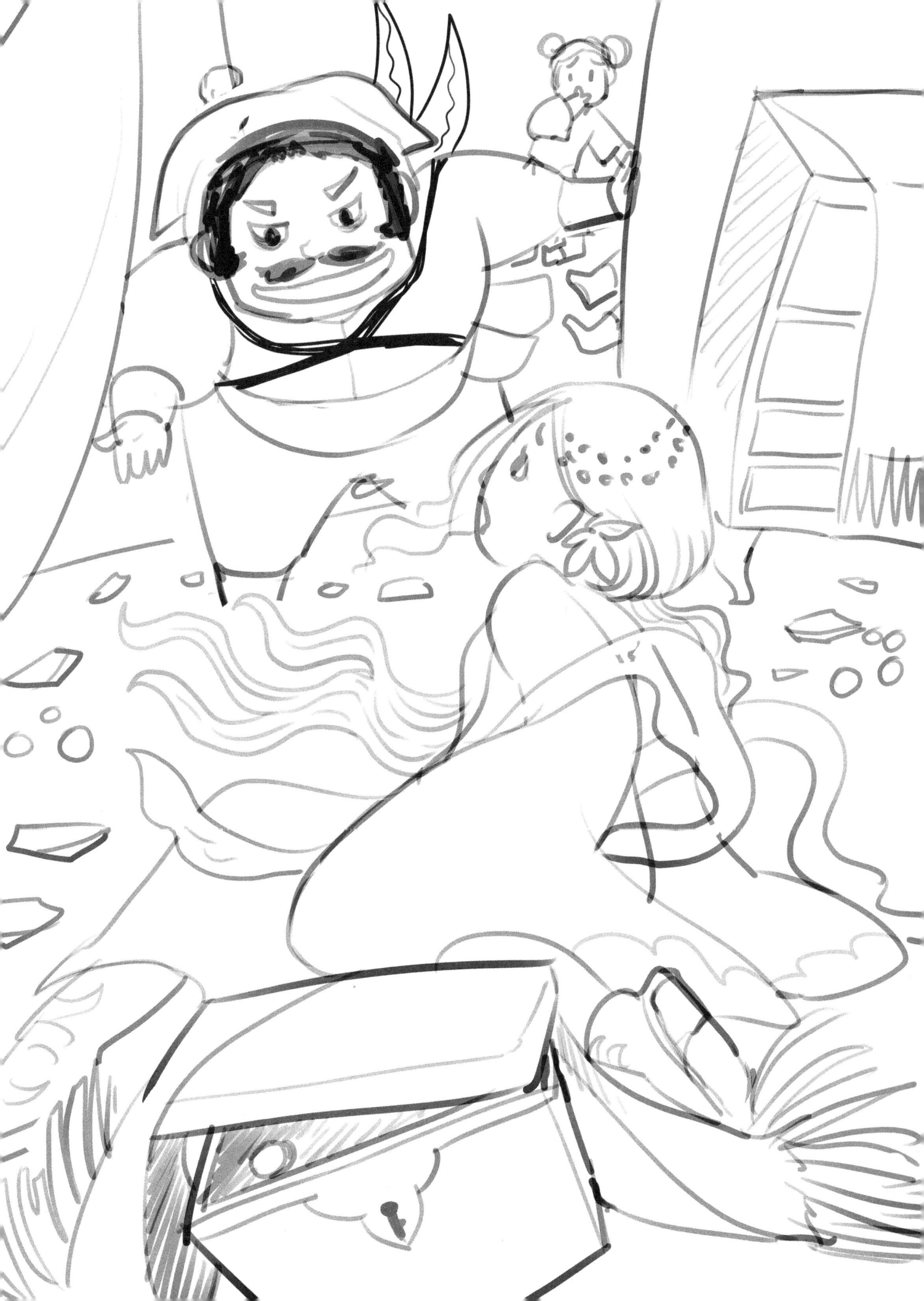

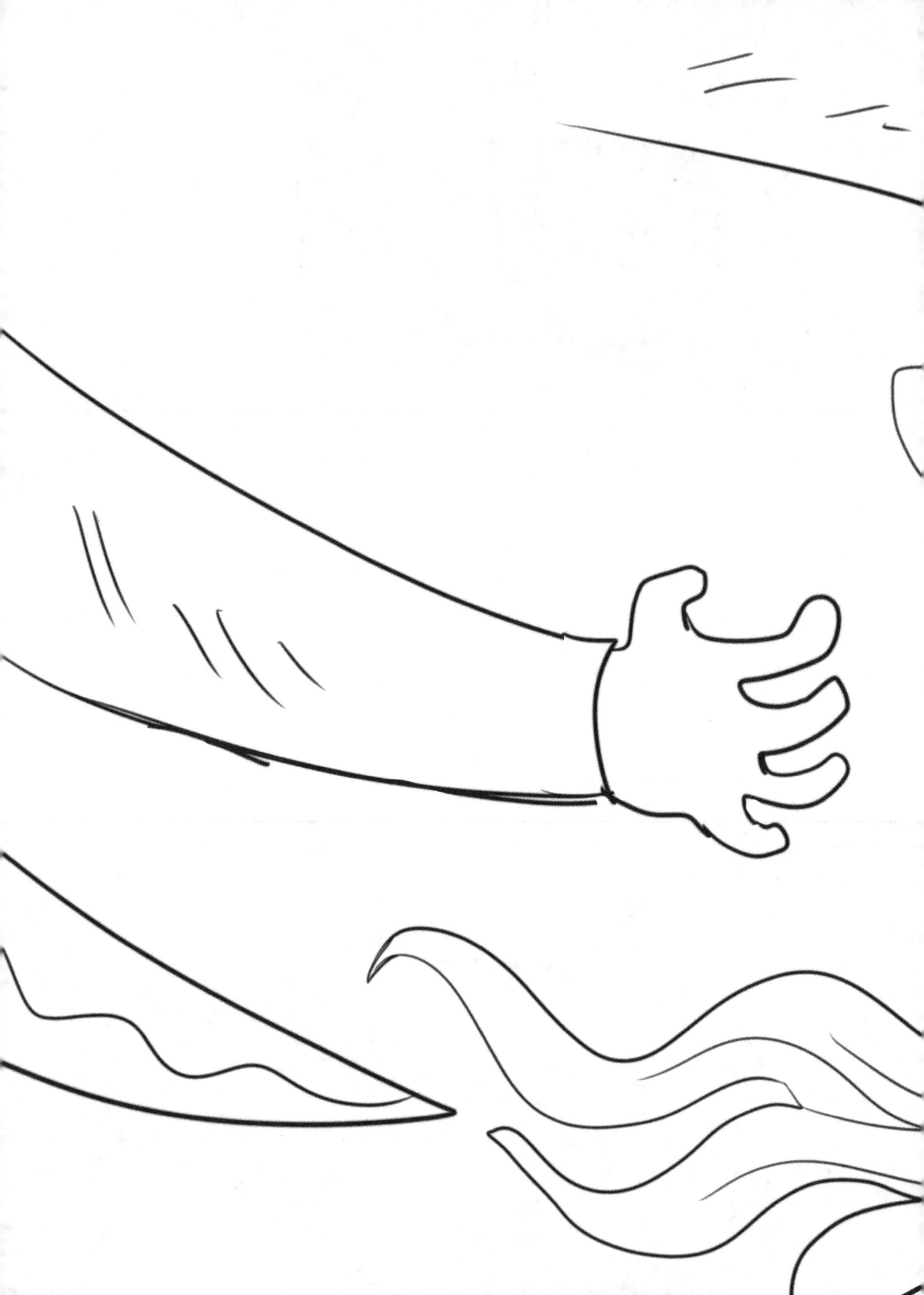

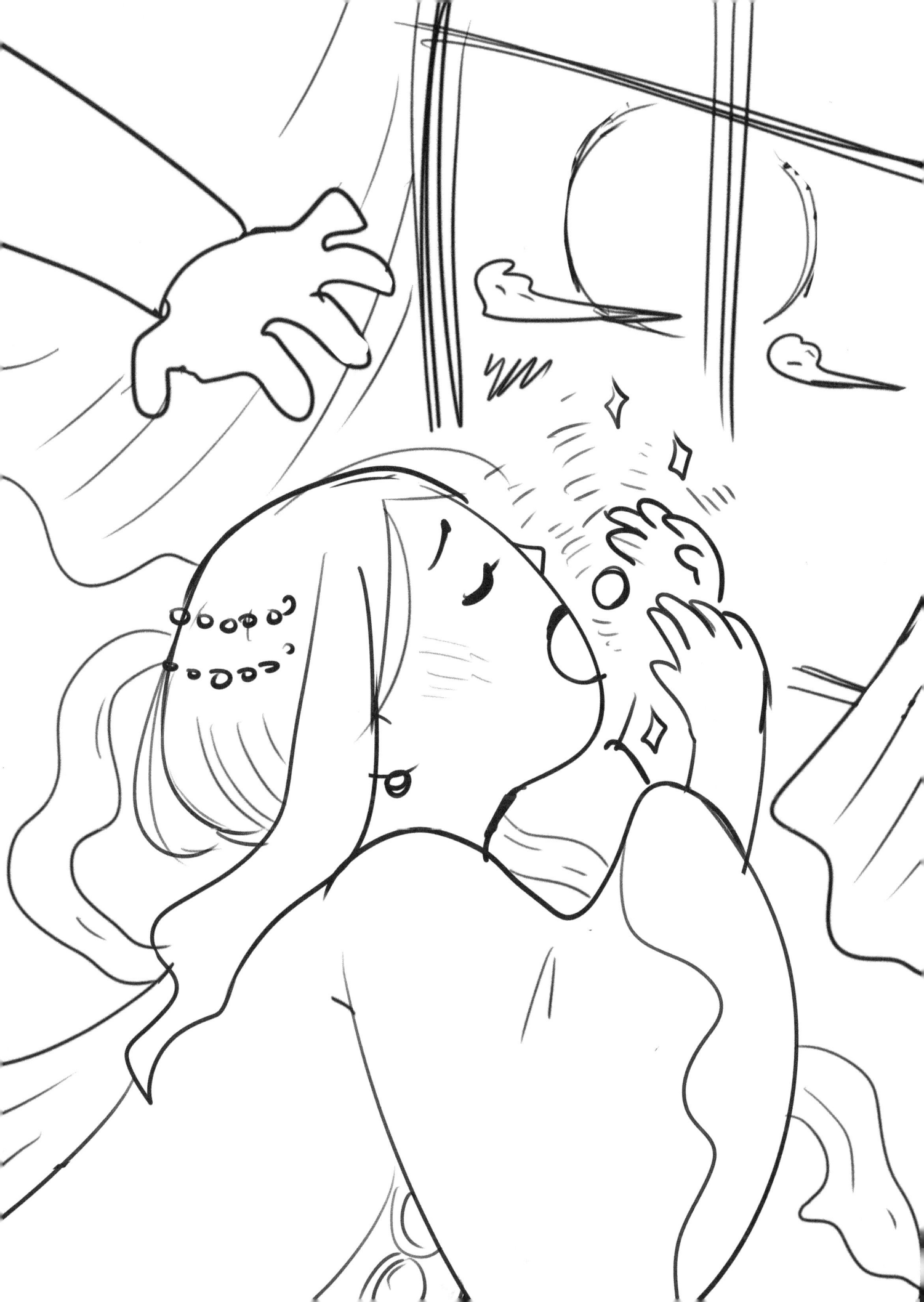

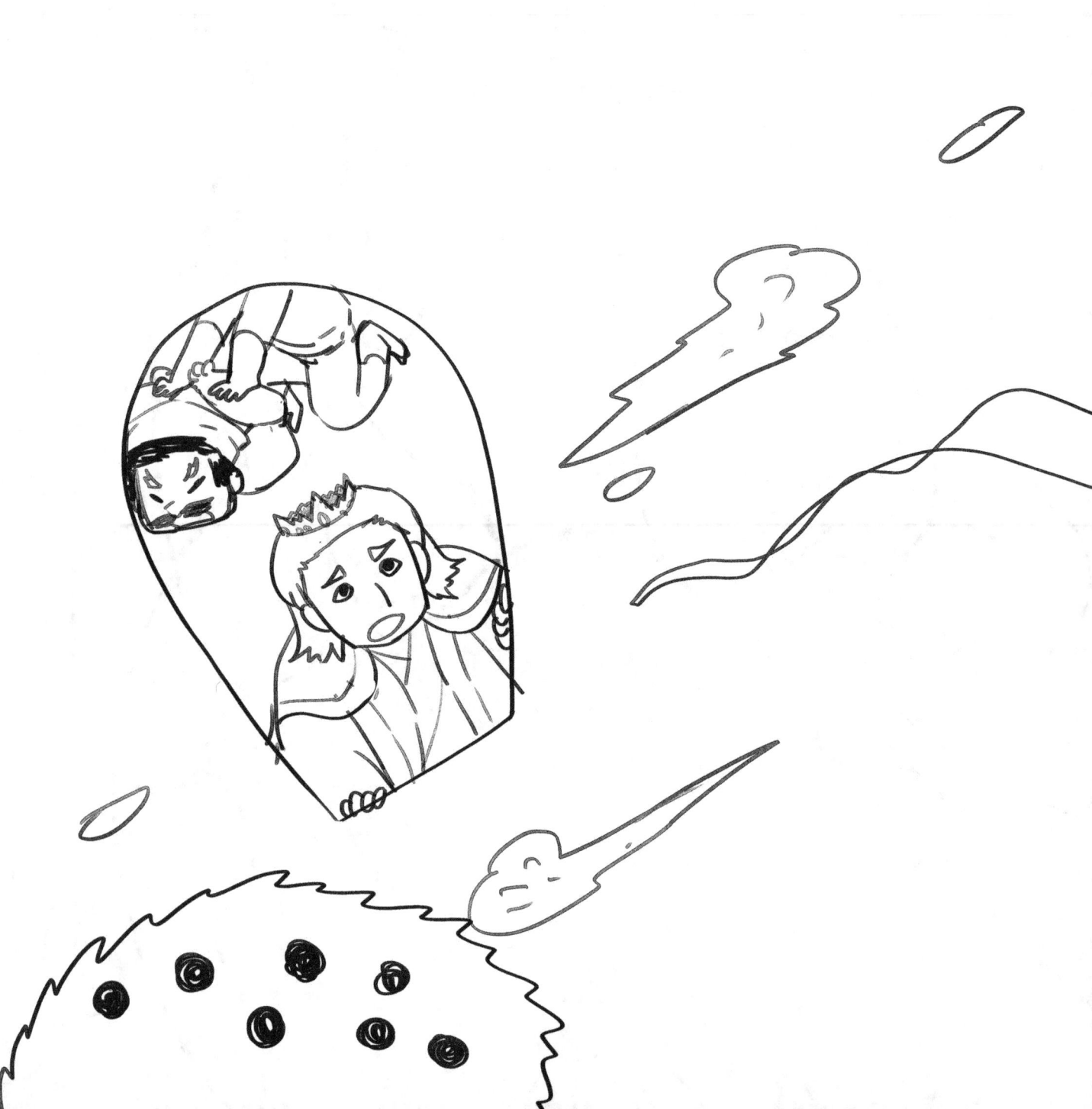

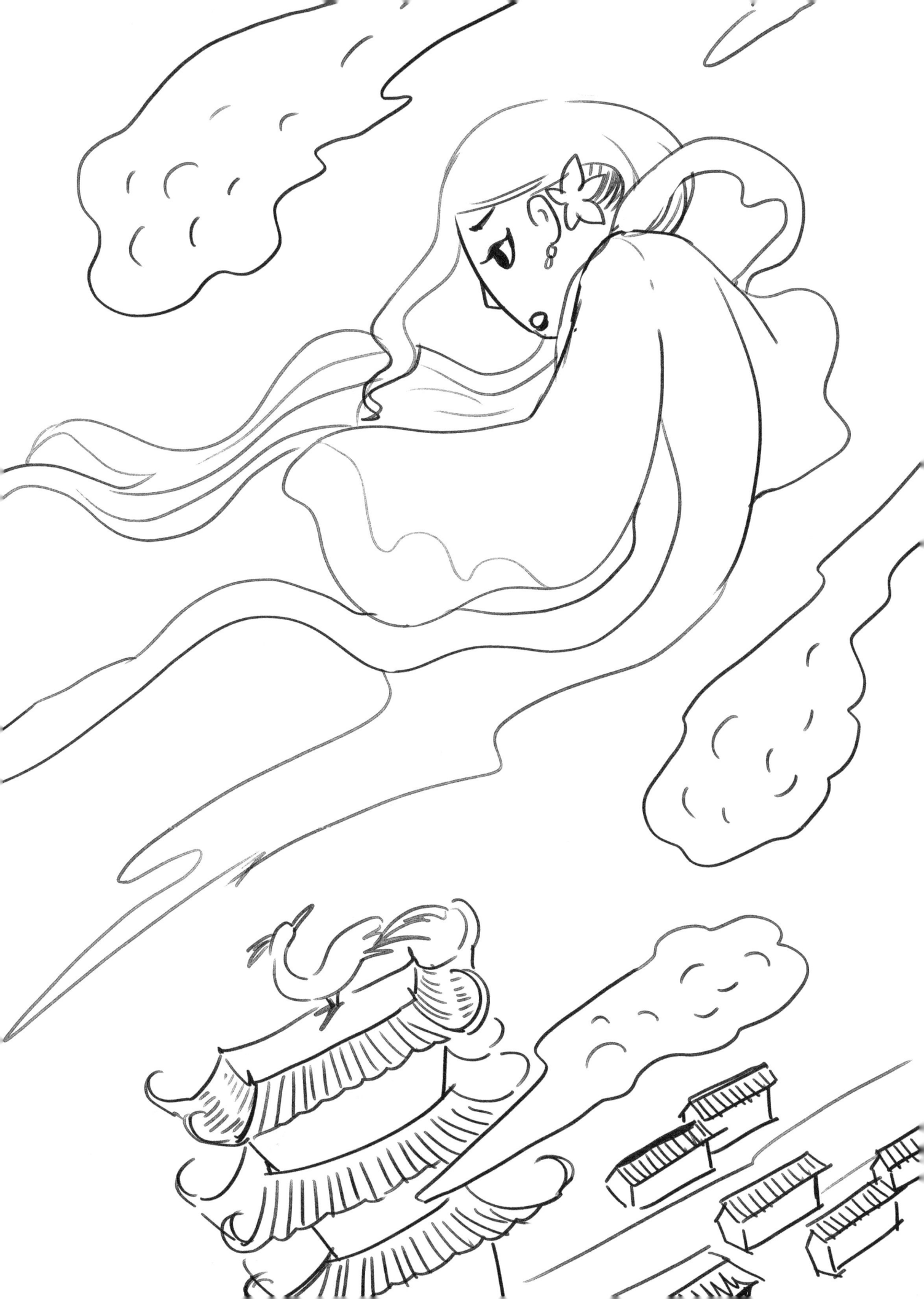

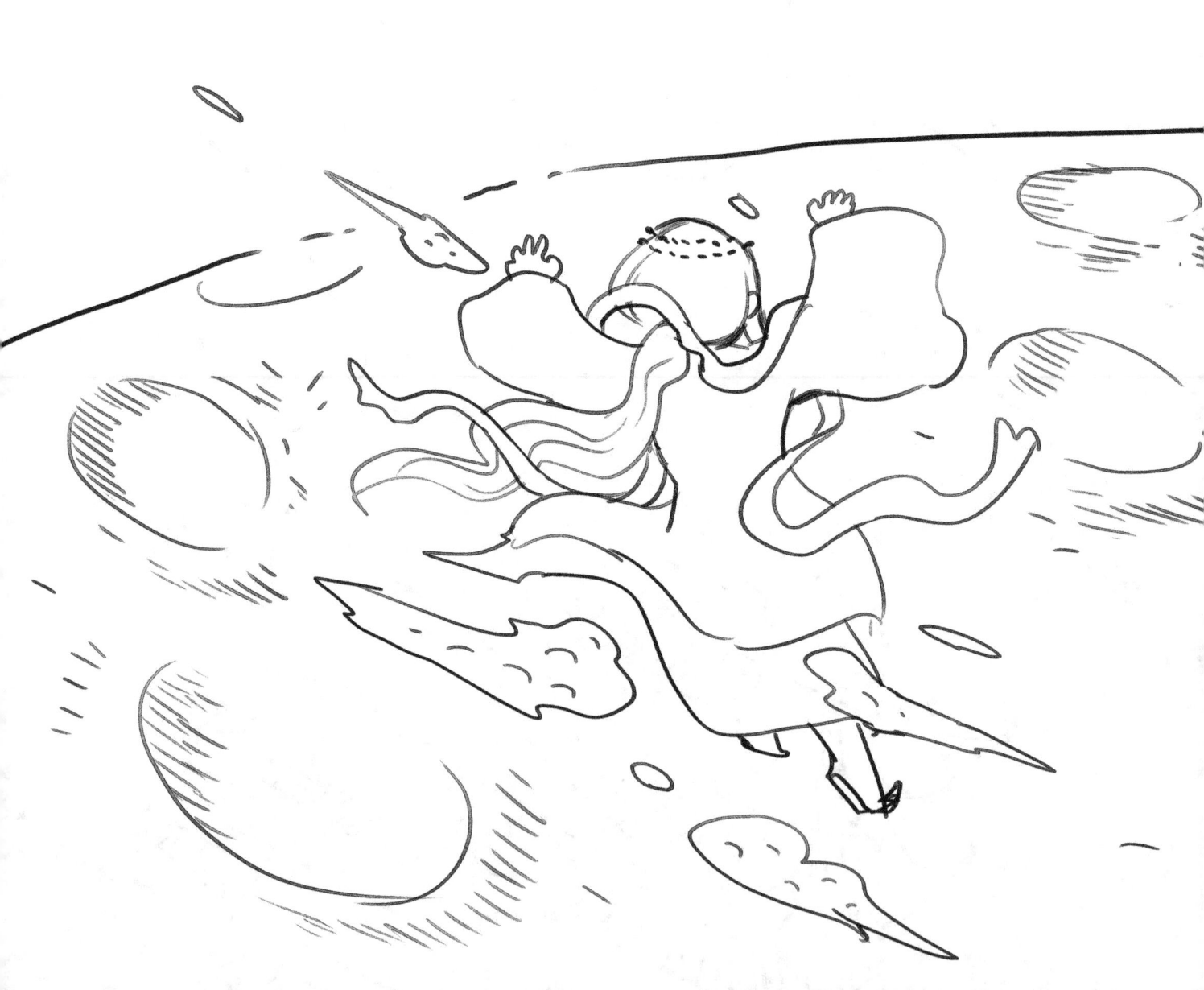

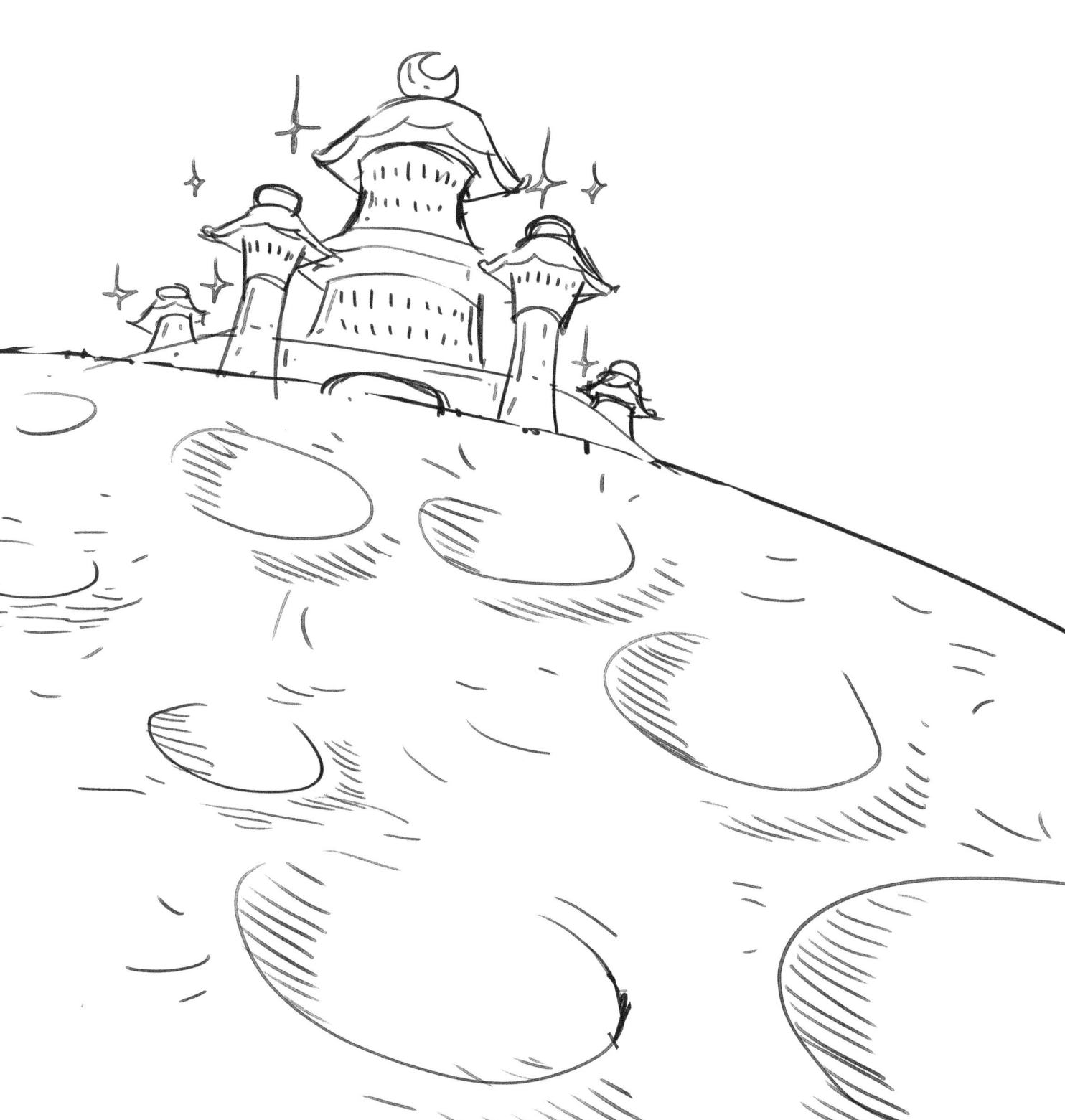

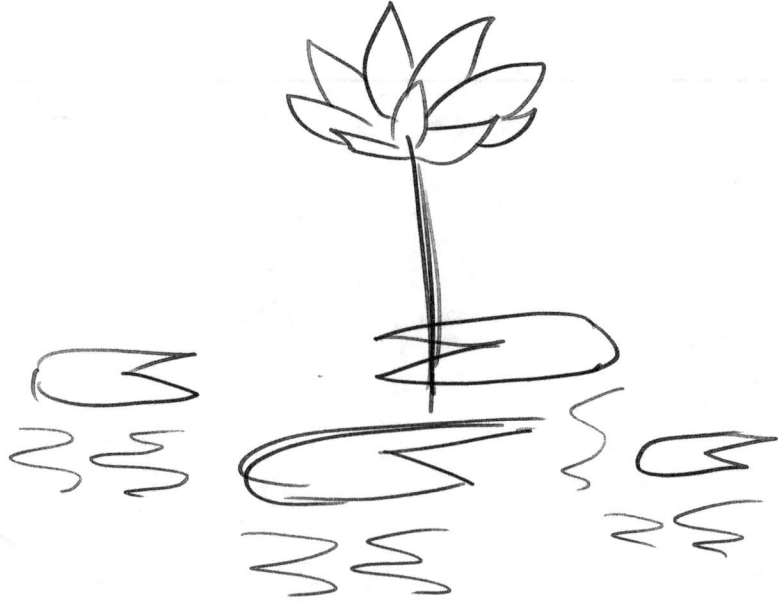

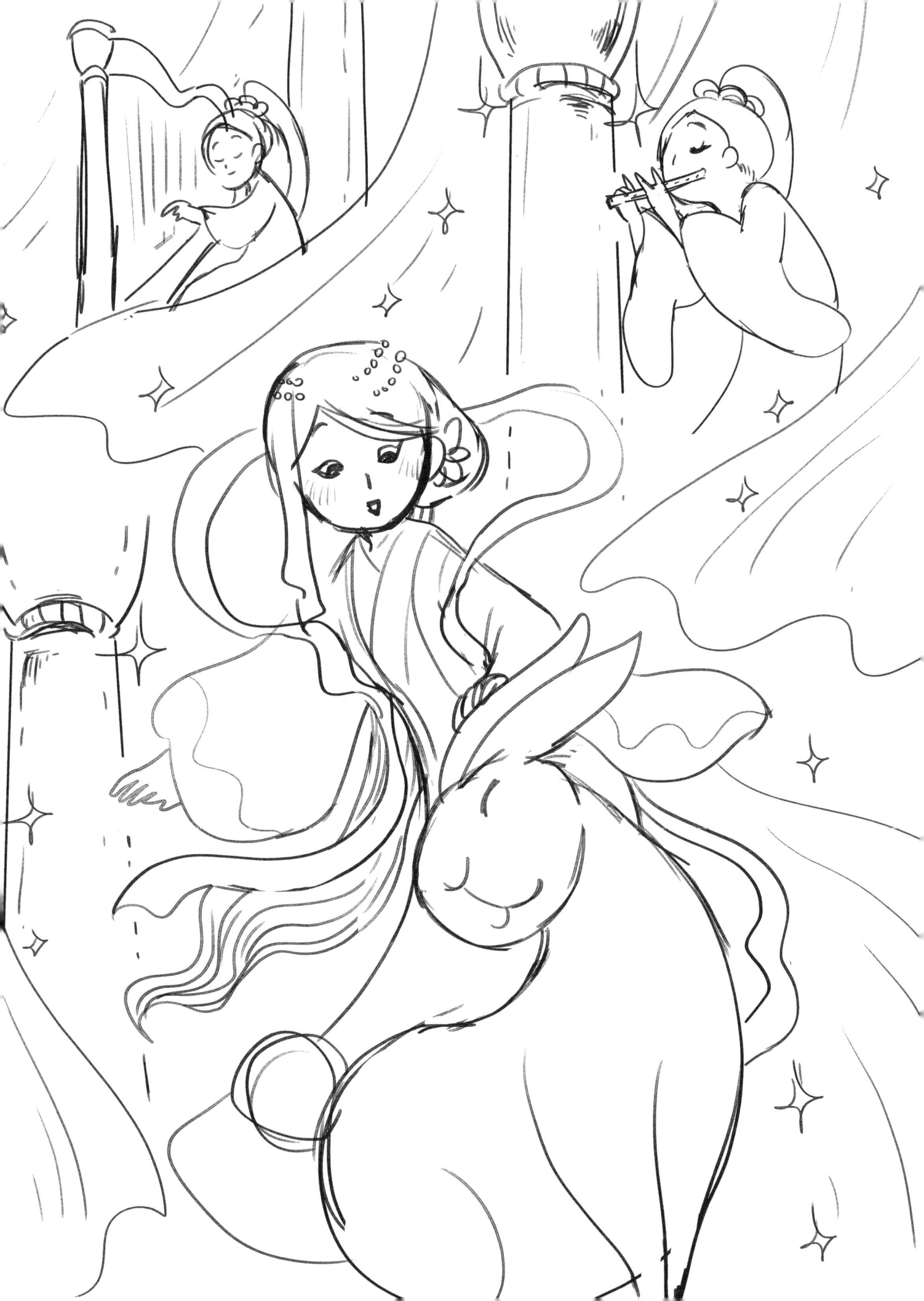

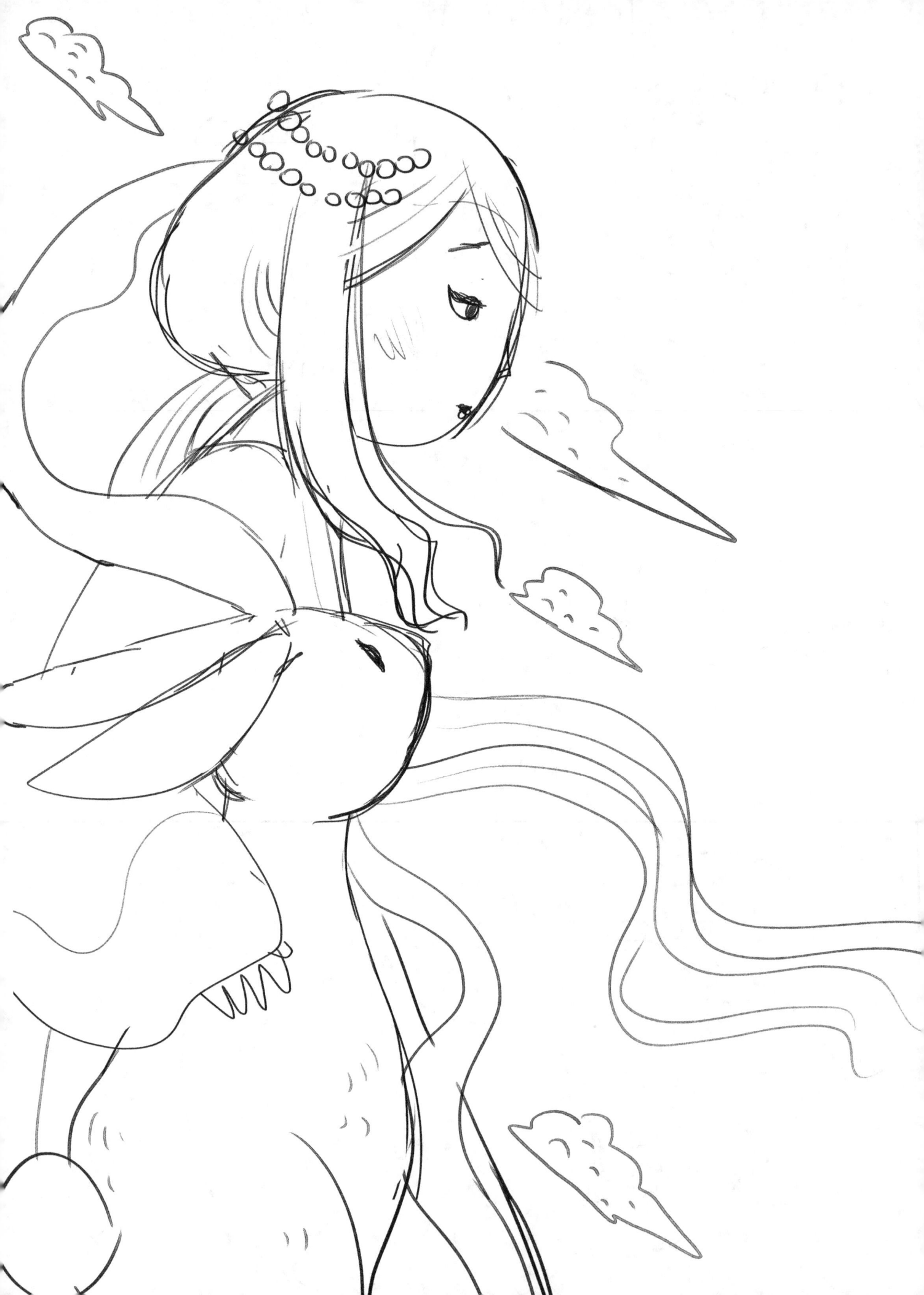

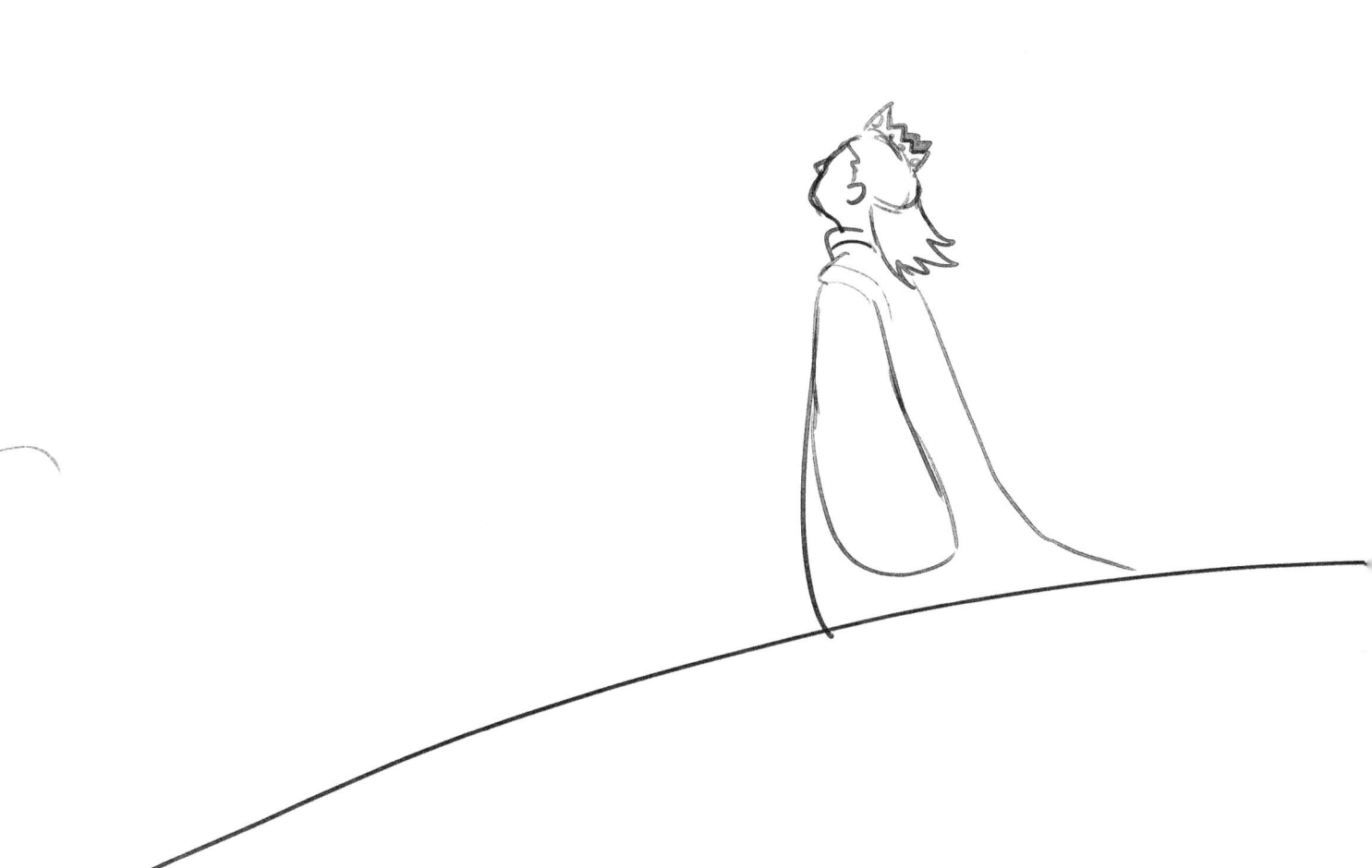

PART TWO

SECTION 1

SECTION 1

SECTION 2

SECTION 2

SECTION 3

SECTION 3

SECTION 4

SECTION 4

SECTION 5

SECTION 5

SECTION 6

SECTION 6

SECTION 7

SECTION 7

SECTION 8

SECTION 8

SECTION 9

SECTION 9

SECTION 10

SECTION 10

SECTION 11

SECTION 11

SECTION 12

SECTION 12

SECTION 13

SECTION 13

SECTION 14

SECTION 14

Appendix
Story of "Princess in Moon"

Section 1

Long-time age, Kingdom "Sha" is a very wealthy kingdom in the old East Continent.

Princess "Astrid" is the youngest daughter of the old King.
Astrid has beautiful eyes and long hair.
Her body has a faint pleasant smell.

Where Astrid appears, there is always laughter.
King and nationals like Astrid very much.

Section 2

When Astrid grow up,
Many young princes from different countries wish to get married to Astrid.

But in the deep heart, Astrid loves the prince "Herman" only.

Section 3

Prince Herman is so handsome and strong,
Always full of vitality and energy.

When he is hunting in the forest, Herman encounters Astrid.

Herman falls in love with Astrid at a glance, so does Astrid too!

Section 4

One day, ten suns appear in the sky suddenly.
Ten suns stay in the sky for several months.

The wind is getting hotter.
The land is crack.
The river is dry.

The people suffer.

Section 5

The Sha's old king announce:
「The man, who can solve this problem,
will be the new king of Sha and princess Astrid will marry him. 」

Many young princes propose many suggestions,
but no one can solve this problem.

Section 6

At this moment, Herman comes forward.
Raise his bow and arrow, point to sun,
Shoot the suns in the sky one by one.

The sun got shot to become a big bird.

Nine arrows shoot nine suns.

Nine suns become nine big birds
disappearing in the sky.

Section 7

One sun leave in the sky only.

The world becomes normal, as usual.

People cheer loudly.
Herman becomes the new king of Kingdom Sha.
Astrid becomes his queen.

Herman and Astrid live a happy life in the palace for few years.

Section 8

The immortal gives Herman one elixir as reward to save the suffering of the people.

The Immortal tells Herman, whoever eats the elixir can be immortal.

Herman collects this elixir carefully in secret place.

Only Herman and Astrid know this secret place.

Section 9

But this caused Prince "Monka" very jealous.

One day, when Hernan is not in the palace.

Monka sneaks into the palace.
Monka try to force Astrid to tell the secret place,
where the elixir is hidden.

Section 10

Astrid is afraid of Monka to get the elixir.
Because Astrid knows if Monka gets the elixir,
Herman will be defeated and killed.

Monka is close to Astrid step by step.
Astrid is no way to run.

Without thinking,
Astrid swallows the elixir.

Section 11

Suddenly, Astrid flies up and up to the sky.

Herman receives the report and rush back to the palace.
Herman catches Monka, but find that Astrid has already flown in the sky.

Herman shouts the name "Astrid" on the ground.
Astrid shouts the name "Herman" in the sky.

But Astrid flies too high.
They cannot hear each other's shouts.

Section 12

Astrid flies higher and higher.
She reaches the Moon.

Astrid finds there is a beautiful crystal palace on the moon.

Section 13

The moon palace have beautiful flower,
clear pool and wonderful fairy music.

There is also a white rabbit named "Jades."

Everything looks so nice.

Section 14

Astrid feels happy and sad.

Astrid knows that she saves Herman.
But Herman cannot stay beside her now.

Astrid only can watch the earth from the moon.
Wait for Herman come to her

Someday in the future…

Do you like this story?

The paperback book and ebook of
" Princess in moon" for this story is available now!
You can compare the color by yourself.
Maybe your painting is better than we do.

Buy the paper book or ebook of the storybook " Princess in moon" now.

Check the following QR code for more information.

The Coloring book of
"Princess in Moon" storybook
Design and finish your style storybook now.

Author: Floyd Franklin

Illustrator: Miao Lin

www.ingramcontent.com/pod-product-compliance
Lightning Source LLC
Chambersburg PA
CBHW081536220526

45467CB00010B/3213